A Little Red String

Claire Richards

BookLeaf Publishing

India | USA | UK

Presentation by *BookLeaf Publishing*

Web: www.bookleafpub.com

E-mail: info@bookleafpub.com

ISBN: 9789358737875

First edition 2023

*For those of you who found words on a
page to be easier than people.*

Women

History is full of powerful women
but we aren't the ones who wrote it.

Hera's rage tore through more than Zeus ever
could.
Aphrodite started a war with her beauty.
Persephone wasn't stolen,
she ran;

why be just a maiden,
when she could be a queen
with a crown made from death itself.
Pomegranate juice looked too much like blood
dripping from that grin,
bringing even Hades to his knees.

Sappho was only found in fragments,
her work destroyed.
Cleopatra wasn't beautiful
but no man wanted to admit defeat,
not to a woman.
So seduction was claimed.

Anne Bonny and Mary Read were pirates,
lovers.

They dressed as men
then showed their chest
before killing those they stole from.
Their victims knew
they were killed by a woman.

Giulia Tofana was executed in 1659
after confessing to helping kill
more than six hundred men.
She supplied poison
to women wanting escape
from an abusive man.

The first Queen Elizabeth reigned
for forty five years
without a husband.
She refused to marry.
She refused to give up her power.
She was the daughter of a strong woman;

a woman who only appears in history as one of
six.
Six women with their own stories.
Stories that aren't told
by any of the history books
because despite all these women
history has always been his story.

Storm

When a single drop falls
nobody blinks.
When a few drops follow
nobody thinks
there is a reason to worry.

But when the thunder strikes
people stop.
When the rain starts to pour
people will listen.

So shout.
Scream.
Thunder gets their attention
but make sure your words can keep it.

Because thunder isn't the force of nature
that helps things grow.
The rain that follows
That is what we will show.

Beauty

By definition
beauty is a combination.
Shapes and colours
that please the aesthetic senses.

Based on this,
one's beauty is defined by one's appearance
but beauty is so much more than one's
appearance
and so much more dangerous than they would
have you believe.

Beauty is a tool.
It is a weapon.
It is the way one holds themselves.
The confidence
in the way they walk,
in the way they talk.

It is the spark in their eyes
and the smile you won't see
when they know they have what they want.
Beauty is the betrayal
you will never see coming.
To you, we were just another pretty face.

So, go ahead.
Underestimate me.
You'll see you're mistake when I am done.

Half Remembered Dreams

In the silent whispers
and the half remembered dreams
is where you will find her.

She sits between
the broken hearts
and empty promises
cleaning the blood from her knuckles.

Hope is not the timid girl
they all believe.

She is the shaky breath
after they tear you down.
She is the dirt on you face
when you stand against them.

Hope is the hand
that pulls you up after
and hands you the match
to watch them all burn.

Angel

There's an angel on the corner.
He sits alone.

If you look closely,
you can see what remains of his halo;
you can see the drops of red in his hair
left by those foolish enough to think they could
fix it.

If you look closely,
you can see where his wings once were;
you can see the stumps left behind
charred to ensure they don't grow back.

Those brave enough to ask,
they know the story.
This was not the work of God.
This was us.

We tore away his innocence
set fire to the remains.
We shattered the good in him
left it as a reminder.

To those who rush past,

there's an angel on the corner.
To those who look closely,
he's not an angel anymore.

What We Find in the Dark

It brings fear,
comfort too,
and sometimes both.
Our minds play games with the shadows.
We forget what is real.

So, we close our eyes
letting the darkness take over.
We can breathe.
The darkness,
it brings relief.

But then we see the shadows.
They flicker,
they move,
they reach,
they pull.

Our eyes snap open.
We come back to the truth.
We realise what it was.

All those shadows
our thoughts.
Tricks playing in our heads.

We close our eyes to bring us comfort
but the demons are still there.
Be careful how long you stay in the dark.

Monster

There is something in the night
that is so much calmer than the day.
There is something in the dark
that is so much nicer than the light.

They said stay away from the darkness,
that's where the monsters are
but what they don't tell you
is that the monsters in the dark are there for a
reason.
The monsters in the dark know
that the monsters in the light are so much more
dangerous.

Things We Lost

If I gave you a box
with all you had lost,
what would it contain?

If I gave you a chest
with all you had left,
What would remain?

If you could take back
what you gave up
would you pick up that innocence,
or would you still choose to suffer
knowing where you end up?

Not Enough

How did we get here my dear?
When did it get so hard?
We used to think we could take the world
but then the world took us.

We are too young to be this tired.
They say we are too young to have a reason to
be
but even when the rest of me stops,
my head can't seem to.

I thought I knew enough.
I don't know it all
but I thought I knew enough.
Oh, my dear, why wasn't it enough?

Conversation Between a
Head and a Heart

I was told to listen to you.

I know.

I was told that you wanted what you wanted,
I was told that you knew best.

I know.
I'm sorry.

Don't be.
It's not your fault
people always try to pin us against each other.
It's not your fault
you trust and love so easily.

It's not your fault that you don't.

I know.

I'm sorry.

I'm sorry too.

Stars

Do you think the stars get lonely
up there all by themselves?

Billions,
trillions,
more stars than we could ever comprehend
fill up a night sky.
Diamonds scattered by the gods,
but oh so alone.

Too many to count.
Too far apart.
Do they miss each other?
Do they miss us?
We sat with them once
a long time ago.

It was too long to remember
but the evidence is there
in the elements we a made from,
in the star light in our eyes,
in the cosmic dust in our veins.
We were stars once too.

Do you think the stars get lonely?
I know I sometimes do.

Lose Them

I've never lost someone
but I'm still missing them.
I've never loved someone
but I can still feel them.

I don't know if I will ever look at someone
and have it hurt when I can't anymore
but I want to.
Because you have to have someone
before you can lose someone.

Maybe If

If I could get away
just for a day
and go anywhere in the world,
maybe I would come home to you.

In a world
of ifs and maybes,
if I ever meet you,
would you maybe stay?

If We Could

Why is there an 'if' in life?
Life gave us what it could.
Could we understand it if we knew,
knew what life wanted to say.
Say what you want,
want what you wish you had.
Had I not asked for it,
it would not be what it is now.
Now life is sure to tell,
tell me a truth.
Truth be told of life,
life will always have an if
if life is what we decide.

Secret

Tell me a secret.
Any kind.
If you don't have a secret,
then tell me a lie.
Tell me something
you could never know.
Tell me where we all go.

Tell me a secret.
I promise I won't say.
If you asked me to,
I wouldn't speak another day.
Darling for you
and only you,
I would do it all.

Tell me a secret.
I now see you can't.
So, I will tell you one of mine,
one I knew from the start.
I saw you and I loved you
and that terrified me
because when I saw you and I loved you,
I saw who I could really be.

Forever

Oh, my love,
forever is a sweet lie
but I would lie to myself forever
if it meant I could spend forever loving you.

Little Red String

Everybody has a story.
A tale only theirs
that they choose the form of.

Mine is a little black book,
full fragments of the same story,
connected by a little red string
only I can see.

But this story starts
between the pages of another.
I am the fabrication
of every word
on every page
in every book I have ever read.

I am found in the narratives
living on the shelves
of my bedroom walls,
held together by that little red string.

We are defined
by the words we write
and in a little black book,
bound by a little red string,
are the words that define me.

Writing is many things
to many people
and I'm still working
on letting this little red string be seen
but for those who have read this far
here is what writing is to me.

Message to Next

To those who come next
I wish you the best,
but I have to say sorry.

We didn't mess this world up.
We tried our best to fix it
but we haven't done enough.

So, to those who come next
I wish you the best.
Good luck with what is left.